American Wild

for the Little Wild Things

What is a Little Wild Thing?

I am not oppressed

I'm just a little kid

who
wants
a chance
to do her best

Like a warrior wind moves waves
to untangle the bisons fierce tress,
neither can I be stopped from seeking my own quest

♥

I am not a victim of early times

I'm just a little kid

who
seeks
our history -
not hides

Like a deer sipping from a coveted stream
under an apricot dawn,
it will keep me from being blind
so in vain zig zags the snake to frighten me
from moving forward,
its slither unable to hypnotize me from seeing
that our stars do shine

♥

I do not hate any color nor black or white
I'm just a little kid

who
respects
all cultures
including mine

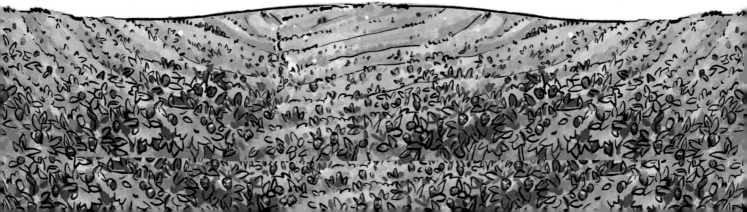

Like rows of rolling strawberry fields,
it is the bright red that beats within
that makes us one of a kind
Unlike animals we have the Word
and that is the trait
that honors our hearts, shapes our character,
and opens our eyes and mind

I am not weak nor brainwashed

I'm just a little kid

enlightened
by
the grace,
the grasp,
the largesse of
His Rod

Like the noble horse in the pasture bows,
perseverance in his nod,
I, as well, find calm in the open prairie,
in the strength of our founding,
One Nation Under God

♥

I am not flawed or anonymous
I'm just a little kid

who
cherishes
bouncing baby boys
and
rosy cheek girls
as
auspiciousness

Like the cobalt skies that hover above turbulent seas,
Protect this innocence
for the birthright of Little Wild Things
will not be cast away as insignificant

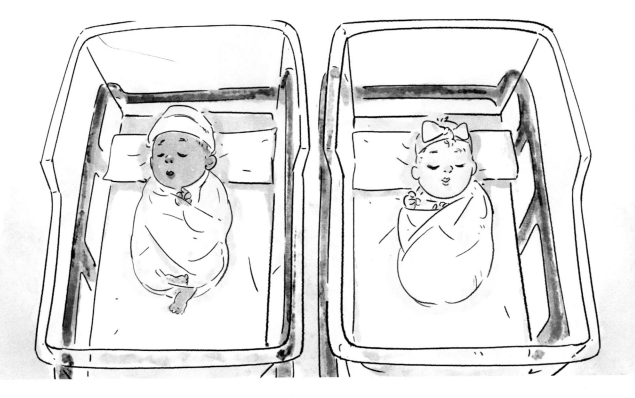

I am not filled with angry thought

I'm just a little kid

resolved

to

find happy

in his spot

Like a bitter frost that rode in from the north,
maybe you forgot -
discern the seasons ire they spread south, east & west
and all for naught

I am not spoiled rotten
I'm just a little kid

who
treasures
my trunk of gifts
overflowing from
the breadth of freedom

Like the Tree of Liberty,
water me in the belief of this incredible dream
for what foes and monsters could not hither,
is the Little Wild Thing's branch to all who seek
its wisdom

I am not owed anything by this world

I'm just a little kid

who
understands
riches are
what I produce
using
my very own free will

Hence was the forethought in our founders herald:
life, liberty, and the pursuit of happiness
belong to all who share upon this soil

I do not wear a frown
I'm just a little kid

aware
that many of valor
preceded me
to overcome
a tyrannical crown

Like mellow apples bend the branches in the orchard
and lace the soft ground,
it is an immeasurable chance they wielded
to plant the seed
that would blossom into a harvest
that escaped the scent of the hound

♥

I am not a pawn in a game of chess
I am a little kid

who
will stand
as tall as I can
in allegiance with my flag
and those who defend
how high it has risen

Like the bee sting before the honey
from the cedar tree flows,
we did make progress
A world was in turmoil, yet from the wild
our Constitution was conceived and thus
the greatest symbol of independence

♥

And
I am not just any little kid.

I am not solitary
I am
from
a family
who is
the peers of Kings

Like wild lilies that sway in the woodsy breeze
We are the people
the American Wild
rooted in this grandeur country

♥

So wouldn't it be fair to wake me every day -
proud
of how far we came against all odds
and where we are now ?

Start telling me stories of our sovereignty and
make a vow ~
US
together
will
outrace
and lasso
the dark clouds

Like the galant birdsong
"I
will
unite
with anybody
to do right
and with nobody
to do wrong"

This harmony cascades above
the fountain of knowledge ever long
and if you allow me listen, I will take flight
and aspire to be wise and strong

♥

American Wild,
though battled and scarred,
rose out of many ~ One

While others still play a
tug of war
pulling to and fro
a vine full of thorns -
Little Wild Things
transcend the dusk for
"you are not judged by
the height you have
risen
but from the depth you
have climbed"
to reach the stars

Born of freedom fighters
Vessels of hope
Inalienable resilience in our spirit

I am an American Child

Sprouted from the rugged stems of the

American Wild

"I would unite with anybody to do right and with nobody to do wrong."

"You are not judged by the heights you have risen, but the depth you have climbed."

~Frederick Douglass

Made in the USA
Columbia, SC
02 March 2022

56787718R00022